Praise for *Groom*

How splendid it is to encounter a book of such refinement that also understands so intimately that the kingdom of poetry is a land of mixed feelings, and that the best poems are not occasions for moral arousal; they are the documentation of intellect, an aesthetic sensibility and the writer's linguistic prowess as it engages in the work of soul-making. But the task Segrest takes up here is an arduous one, as it explores the line between damage and desire, affection and manipulation, and the poems don't give us easy answers. In fact, they provide no answers at all; instead they ask questions of the deepest and most profound order: how much of the self is our own creation? How much of the self is made of what has been done unto us? I am enamored of Austin Segrest's *Groom* for its brilliance, its discernment, its broken, golden and tenderly reconstructed heart.

Mark Wunderlich, author of *God of Nothingness* and *The Earth Avails*

An honest poet is rare. *Let me not deceive me,* implores our speaker in this astonishing and honest collection from Austin Segrest. *The past is slippery.* Honesty is rendering people, places, things, and ideas with the dignified complexity they require. Honesty is different from truth, did you know? Not unlike it, Segrest asserts that *freedom and respect must be earned.* At times, it must be *taken.* Hewn from life, from hard-won half-knowledge, the phonic echoes, sense details, and calibrated pacing of these poems transport us from caves in northern central Alabama to Damascus, they bring us far into the interior of bewildering and bewitching beloveds, and by the time they return us — *wet leaves out of nowhere / turning back to soil* — we arrive at new understanding of what it means to be *chosen / as the object / of attention.* In attending, and objecting, Austin Segrest brings into our hands a chance to go back on all we thought was right, and as our speaker ardently, honestly claims, *It was right.*

Paul Tran, author of *All the Flowers Kneeling*

Dearly beloved, we are gathered to witness the chimerical unions of thought and feeling displayed in Austin Segrest's latest intensity, his second poetry collection. The title, *Groom*, is noun and verb, passive and active, a pliable hero topping a three-tiered cake. These poems bear a classical weight with the candor of intimate conversation, and find beauty in the wreckage of Gen X's suburbia. Who here hasn't acted against their own best interest in search of something that might answer to the word "love," only to find the *contempt a host / harbors for the one guest who showed*?

Gregory Pardlo, author of *Spectral Evidence* and *Digest*

Austin Segrest's *Groom* captures an age, a place, and a time with stunning clarity. It is a transformational mapping of *the boundless private* through apartment complexes and parking lots and Birmingham nights spent in the shadow of Vulcan, where secrets, loyalty and desire are weaponized. If you too were a teenager made from a *disproportionate amount ... of night* (and aren't we all?), these poems are essential reading.

Rita Mae Reese, author of *The Book of Hulga* and *The Alphabet Conspiracy*

Presided over by Hermes — god of the crossroads, god who in the same gesture gives and takes — *Groom* is a devastating verse bildungsroman. In another poet's hands, this book might have evolved as a simpler survivor's testimonial. Instead, Segrest marshals his artistry to flay open a relationship where threat feels twinned with rescue. What do these wrenching poems teach us about being groomed? That a boy neglected by his own parents might protect his abuser because he himself feels like *a barter / between silences.* That a child, flattered by an older man, is warmed by *the sweet fire, paler than grass, of being noticed.* That kids let in the back door of an adult sexual world are under the *illusion / of gaining access, / rather than providing it.* Segrest's speaker is wise as well as sadly witty. Comparing his vulnerability to Paul's in Caravaggio's "Conversion on the Way to Damascus," he recognizes that *it was a raised hoof, // not love's roof, / you were raised under.* So why would that boy, now grown, maintain an uneasy contact with his groomer? The poems show us that it's because, once upon a time, the groomer's eyes *when he came home / [were] like a dose of naloxone reviving / lost boys sprawled across his couches. Groom's* spare, sharp, whip-smart language lights up, *like coals in a clamshell,* an intricate abyss of need and trust and betrayal.

V. Penelope Pelizzon, author of *Nostos* and
A Gaze Hound That Hunteth by the Eye

Groom

Groom
Austin Segrest

UNBOUND EDITION PRESS
Atlanta

FIRST EDITION

Printed in the United States of America

LIBRARY OF CONGRESS RECORD

Name: Segrest, Austin, 1980 – author.
Title: Groom / Austin Segrest.
Edition: First edition.
Published: Atlanta : Unbound Edition Press, 2025.

LCCN: 2024946030
LCCN Permalink: https://lccn.loc.gov/2024946030
ISBN: 979-8-9906141-9-2 (fine softcover)

Designed by Eleanor Safe and Joseph Floresca
Printed by Bookmobile, Minneapolis, MN
Distributed by Itasca Books

123456789

Unbound Edition Press
1270 Caroline Street, Suite D120
Box 448
Atlanta, GA 30307

Contents

2/

3/

\

Groom

I have known myself a nephew to confusions

HART CRANE

Prayer to Hermes

You plucked the hundred eyes of Argus
        and stuck them in the peacock's tail.

Turning every way to keep the way,
        you outshift Eden's flaming sword.

Short of a halo, lend me your traveler's hat,
        your cloak for shelter in the heath,

your shoes for wandering among the shades.
        Let me not deceive me (no contrivance

or dream escapes you). O god of wrestling,
        teach me to wriggle and bend,

the holds and the throws. The past is slippery.
        You are the thief at the gates.

1/

The Anarchist Cookbook

\

Steve, though he'd cut you
if you crossed him, drop you like a sack
of potatoes if you came at him drunk
like Randy Parr in the backyard,
Steve had no truck with violence —
no guns, nary a knife that I remember.
But, susceptible to conspiracy,
that bitter pap of the bright
but undereducated, he liked the idea
(and who doesn't?) of having what he shouldn't.
Like when he cooked the books
waiting tables at Red Lobster,
pocketing discounts from coupons
slipped in at the register.
A iittle weed money. A little fuck you.

\

The Cookbook was black, a big paperback,
with just the title blocked in white
at a severe tilt. How to make
tear gas in your basement,
DMT, a chimney trap ...

Devil's Book, Philosopher's stone,
it promised to unleash the miraculous
from the everyday detritus of our lives.
Not that we ever tried a recipe.
I don't remember cooking up
banana peels, or making a paste
to trip on morning glory seeds.

\

Amazing how much of his creed
came out of that book: freedom and respect
must be earned — taken from your parents.
The only laws an individual can obey
are those he instills in himself.
Think about it: who controls the information,
the military manuals Bill Powell freed
from the dust of the public library:
Explosives and Booby Traps, Escape and Evasion.

\

Once I started hanging around,
I put away childish things, homemade
napalm and flamethrowers. I'd gotten behind
the creek's veil. I wanted the fire
inside.
        It ended for most
of the guys who came through me
with leaving for college. With the internet
and the Cookbook — getaway
car literature — more of a badge
than a tool for terrorists. With Columbine,
which brought Bill Powell out
of hiding to condemn the book
he made when he was nineteen.
Steve went on for years
to feed and feed off the lost and ungrateful
and dissipated, making sure,
if nothing else, we couldn't lash out
at a world that never gave us anything.

Brookwood Mall

Dad always said he'd go to Mars.
Couldn't we come? He wasn't happy.
John and I were at the mall,
twelve or so, our bikes heaped
beside the creek. Like a refugee,
Mom had started sleeping in
the extra twin bed pushed up
against mine. I wasn't smart like John.
Hadn't made the basketball team.
We were watching this fountain.
A ring of jets arced into the middle.
What if it was a portal?
Somehow all the miles of creeks
had led to this fountain, this fantasy.
It was the early '90s. In a chatroom sting,
a vice-principal — it could have been
that very afternoon — was nabbed
luring a minor to the mall.
Did they cuff him in the food court?
His polyester forest green?
Before feeding the fountain
(that's how I imagined it), the creek
ran under the overpass, wrapping
around the office building
where Mom would talk to her therapist,
feeding it tears. Then it split
and drank the monied shade (or the shade
drank it) darkening the old brick
school and soccer field where I
had fed it tears of my own.

It cut behind the half-timbered facades
of English Village and grocery,
swinging past Steve's apartment
(I hadn't met him yet, but soon).
From either porch you could see it
recede like a promise.
Then it crossed the golf course,
naked of even a shrub, and passed
within blocks of Mom's beloved
first house after the divorce.
Freefall and free-for-all —
the rickety deck looking down
into the valley burned that first spring
(still to come) with the slow tongue
of bruised white blooms saying jump.

All the Young Dudes

Trap or charity,

who can codify,

whose job is it

to break the horse

(the force

beneath the surface)

of desire? To give it

rein, and rein it in?

Steve cultivated

a nowhere else where

a guy could be

different, out,

escape, experiment.

It was a service.

It was obvious

he got his kicks

in return.

He bragged about us,

I've learned, — *his den*

full of boys — to coworkers

who despised him.

Big Brother

The FBI interviewed me
in Dad's cavernous cookie-
cutter by the high school,
an upstairs shutter askew,
the table glass sticky, the cabinet
doors sagging. Two agents,
I want to say. A notebook. A man
asking questions about Dean,
the vice-principal
nabbed at the mall.
He was my friend's Big Brother
in the Big Brother, Big Sister
Program — the friend who lived
next door to Steve.
We'd gone to Dean's beach condo.
I told the agent what I knew
beforehand: Dean would grab my friend's
junk in the car and squeeze
while he fought him to let go.
We hadn't told anyone.
Why would I go?
We were thirteen.
It was the beach. I was
a buffer, I guess.
Did they know each other,
about each other,
my friend's much older
friends — predators, enablers?

I remember Dean's fancy
camera on the table. My friend and I
roamed the beach, tried to talk
to a girl. He was a live wire, manic,
suicidal, my friend.
We dug a cross he lay in
and prayed. Dean retired
early, not a peep as we pilfered
liquor, jacked off in condoms
in the spare bedroom.
My friend got rowdy,
incoherent, threatening
to jump out the window.
Finally, I decked him.

I didn't tell the feds
any of that. The maids
let themselves in,
avoiding us in the kitchen.
Dad was at the lab,
or in the tub,
nonconfrontational
as Commander Lowell.
I dug in, for some reason
determined not to let them
make anything of Dean
haunting the weight room,
and put them off rumors

of a neighbor, quick.
I was calm, stoic.
Who else did they have,
the Deans and Steves?
I have these dreams
of getting grabbed,
pleading, paralyzed
with pain. Does it matter
I thought I was just as bad?
I was a barter
between silences,
a broker of chances.
In the house of damage
doing damage
control, the screw's thread
disappearing in the board.

Initiation

There was so dense a veil of tangled foliage
about it, that none but a sworn lover
of gloomy recesses would have discovered
the low arch of its entrance.

HAWTHORNE

In north central Alabama, caves
are still being found. Holes
in the ground, holes in the hills —
too many to regulate. He took me
to one from his childhood in Warrior,
along beautiful Locust Fork.
No markers, you climb
an anonymous green hill.

Weirded out, even a little afraid
of this man who'd earlier invited me
into his apartment (already
entertaining two young men,
LDS missionaries in ties,
their bikes leaned against the porch
he shared with my friend),
now showing up at Mom's
boldly seeking me out, I must have felt
like Dad before his LSD experiment.
Depthless dark, getting lost or trapped.

How did he pull it off?
37 to my 14, he looked
my mother in the eye, nice to meet you,
Susan, like a bible salesman,
yes ma'am, something you don't mind
him getting dirty: the ritual
prelude to what wasn't
unlike a first date. He'd gathered
beforehand she was single. Still,
in that reprehensibly reputable
suburb, it was ballsy.

With that trip north in Steve's
stripped-down primer gray pickup,
I was led out (as it was said of girls)
into manhood, given away.
I drove, throwing the long,
soft clutch through four muddy gears.
Of the earthen veins beneath Warrior
so like the capillaries and ducts
he flushed as a dialysis
technician, I remember
graffiti in the first room;
shotgun shells; high and low,
a puzzle of tunnels; a slippery
board above an abyss.

Creek

A to B, the plunge of least resistance.
Quantum route, questing root,
hidden, bidden. No creek is straight,
can assume any shape. Glorified gutter,
convict's covert where you were first
taken, initiate, convert. An opening,
a deepening, a naked body.
Plagiarized, possessed, a word appears
you can rhyme but not define.
Low point, bedrock, favorite channel.
A cast of castaways, O castoff skin
of water. A getting into, a getting away,
or away with. Family defection
arranged in a kind of theater,
a kind of play. Each novel
stretch ritual and revelation.
It follows its own lesson.

On the Road to Damascus

after Caravaggio

A bolt breaks the shade and knocks
        Saul clean off his horse. Unbuckled,
his naked legs are ravished, his cheek and neck
        flushed by the light's concussion.

A coal in a clamshell,
auroral, the faint stubble
at his chin and burning cheek.
        The light strikes his throat white.
The backs of his hands in shadow.

City Brook

Coming down the slope
and into the enclave, the tiny kingdom,

before merging with the seam
running the length of the golf course,

I heard it flowed through a house,
a girl's I never knew, someone's cousin.

A creek I never saw, and a girl I never knew,
and a house I only got a glimpse of

below the street, hidden in the trees,
leaving me looking down from a banister

at it running through the den,
for a moment — before it got exposed

and lost in another body — rainless,
birdless. Its white noise

in every room. Its metallic damp
and grit you can't get in the books,

in all the books.

The Groom

after Caravaggio

The groom's behind the horse,
        turning it back from Saul
in the foreground by the bridle,

his other hand gentle on the soft
        white muzzle.
His balding pate and deeply

rutted, obsequiously bowed brow
        intent on sparing his master — what?
Interruption? Embarrassment?

Getting stepped on? The horse's
        oblique flank shines. And Saul
is bedded down beneath it on his coral

cape. Coral, his nippled breastplate.
        His hands raised wide invert the banner
of the horse's back, rump to lowered

head, making a circle. The horse
        looks back where it had intended
to step. Why couldn't it

see what we see, just in time — what Saul
        sees with closed eyes, like the sun-
bleached eyes of a statue?

Once, in the hollow of a dark
    park, a man I knew and trusted
swooped into a cone of lamplight,

at the last second saving me, he said,
    from a mugging I never saw coming
or going.
                    His bare feet, that vein

down his calf — the groom's legs
    blend with the horse's. It's complicated,
I said once to a survivor, who wasn't

having it. But to disentangle
    even a toe, an ankle — it never fully
resolves, even after you see the hoof

raised over Saul.

Stealth

Bass waves wobbled
under huge, lugubrious licks.

Oversize '90s,
you needed all that room,

all those subwoofers to sublimate,
all that distortion, all those angles

and continuous curvature
to deflect

your failure to thrive
inside the lie

of exponential growth,
the boundless private.

Your wide-open why not, just do it overtop
a brooding tempo creeping to a halt,

before running
back the other way.

You're hard, you're huge, you're jacked.
No Fear, No Limits, No Boundaries,

your bumper stickers bragged.
Taunting the silence.

Allegory

He tears me from the lake. A sudden blow.
For a long time I can't feel his talons,
hanging lank like Zeppelin's Icarus.
The valley inverts his wings.
We circle the buildings
of his mother-complex.
She's making his favorite,
ribs, his high school portrait's
young Bowie features feathered in the hallway,
his peacocks oil slicks my hair drags through.
Falkor and Sebastian at the end of *The Neverending Story,*
we're free of Mom's Slough of Despond and anesthesia awareness,
we're strafing the father poets of the greater south, who run
before us, shaking their fists at the sky, "no threat, no poem!"
We're high and aloof as Dad's brief bachelor pad,
or glider fantasy (what if we need an engine?
Who'll steer?). Until the pain, until we're not,
we're pure as the rumor of Don Juan Johnson's secret
penthouse in that tower in Destin, where once we stayed.
Laid in that white rush.

Hermes

\

In seventh grade I met him
in Mrs. Lawrence's advanced

English. I met the whole lot.
But Hermes, with his herm-

morphic thing — god of many
shapes and shifts, turns and tricks,

of many hats and guises,
thefts and gifts,

dreams and crossings,
of the many changes and exchanges —

\

Nightwatchman and thief,

black root

he steals and keeps

milk white moly

what he steals,

one drug intercepts

the way you can steal

another on its way

that which is given,

to the witch

that which lunges at you.

2/

Celestial Realm

What did Steve look like? I drew him once
in purple colored pencil. Such handsomeness

didn't hurt his chances charming Mom.
Devious green eyes. High cheek

and forehead. Square, smooth jaw, long
lashes, even a bit

of the English beak that runs
on Mom's side of the family.

He passed as straight, or, with a few
touches, a woman (he'd sold coke in drag).

Or, as a relation of mine.
We were in a coffee shop, mid-nineties

pre-Starbucks southside Birmingham,
crowned in clove smoke in a corner.

It was dark roast, big clay mugs, wide
wedges of cake.

He's looking down
at an oblique angle, gap teeth and lashes,

almost bashful (he was anything but).
My pencil struggled with the shadows

of his cut-off sleeves, a dancer's shoulders.
        But I captured something. Joy. First blush,

the ever only successful portrait
        from life in my life: only Steve

could have brought it out. Probably,
        he was drawing, too. Or laying out cards.

Goth girls and baggy grungers milled around
        thrifted couches and recliners

like the furniture in his own den.
        Low reddish lamplight.

                                        Outside,
        Highland Avenue wound the cusp

of Red Mountain. It makes twin
        incursions into folds of the limestone,

describing two declivities, crotch-
        shaped parks, dark now, known for cruising.

Sneaking Out

Roof studs scaffolded the stars.
Mineshaft of night.
Odor of sawdust, plastic, glue —
of making.

Fresh pink rolls of insulation,
bright white PVC.
Nail-glint, coils of wire,
and some bit of metal bent
for a pipe.

The lighter throws its aureole
around our own half-finished
ecstatic adolescent
bodies we couldn't see
anybody wanting,

which, like our illusion
of gaining access
rather than providing it,
made us easier to manipulate.

Revision

after Caravaggio

In this version, the voice
is Paul's speaking back to Saul

about what he saw

when the scales fell off —

not days, but years,
decades, after.

At love's command you lay down

under the raised hoof.

If not for him, you wouldn't have
been in that park, or Atlanta.

There was a blind spot

where your knowing was concerned:

taking for granted that you, too,
would never get to not know.

And so you didn't.

You lay beneath the voice

telling you, you count, you're special.
His power over you,

his banner:

it was a raised hoof,

not love's roof,
you were raised under.

Steve's Bed

Pink Floyd's *Animals*
drones through a thin
dreamless sleep I keep
waking from to see the
quartz lock's molten
glow on his dresser
pierce the dark like Vulcan's
torch lit over the city.
The sheets are dark satin.
I'm in my boxers with
my back to him, in need
and afraid. The lulling
acoustic's punctured like
a deflated lung with electric
dread, like the eternal
last lingering of a trip.
Pig grunt. Bleating. A one-
hitter plugged with shwag.
It only takes a little, he
likes to say, closing his eyes
and singing a bar, each
Hammond octave a decade
long. "And when you lose
control," Gilmour sings,
"you'll reap the harvest
you have sown." And remember
this bed, cherished among
troubled boys like a parent's,
taking a hit before lying
back, a sip of his sweet tea —
he who never turned you out,
you, who never let him.

Behind the Curtain

No one talked
about Black people —

        janitors and housekeepers

kept behind the wall.

He loved Black people,
but didn't need any

undo attention

        around his place.

In Mountain Brook's refusal
to bus or incorporate,

        to countenance

anything but the invisible

labor of Black people
kept behind the curtain

of Red Mountain,

        in that ethos,

the seed
of our rebellion.

Land Line

I'd forgotten phones, all the times we must have talked on the phone —
dial tones, hitting the hook switch. Where was his?
Curling from his kitchen wall, or cordless on the dark
glass Randy fell through in the den? A red eye
charging in its cradle?

Would I talk on the big button phone, standing at the shelf
in my sister's basement room,
the closer to the sliding glass door it was
gratuitous to say I snuck out?
I'm sure I had my own, a new one for Christmas,

as we had our own rooms and people, so that calling
him was a kind of calling home. Even weirder,
that he would have called me, chatting me up on the common line,
risking going through my mom, sister, brother.
Austin there? — Hey. — Hey, whatcha doin?

bubbly, almost laughing, like he's at a party dancing,
and where was I?
                                        Later, stopped short

I would have done the calling. Hoping
for the green light. Afraid

he wasn't there, or wouldn't answer, or wouldn't be there
if he was, his patience (having gotten — having not
gotten what he wanted) having thinned
like an old pair of scrubs, resentment creeping in-
to the line like mold in his tiny bathroom, tiled

in the forties for maids: he had enough
patients as it was — impinging on his sciatica
and hemorrhoids, robbing him of sleep.
Hating myself in his flat *uh-huhs,* his sighs and silence
and fits of pique, *so you coming over or what?*

Grammar

\

There's a case for giving
and a case for taking away.

He gave x [*to me* — dative]
He took y [*from me* — ablative]

These are the hardest to keep straight
and sometimes take the same form.

\

DA
Datta: what have we given?

from *do, dare,* to give,
with Derridian

traces of dote,
dare, date, Dad.

\

AB

Lative: what have we lost?

from *ab*, meaning *from*
+ *lative*, not from

latere, to lie
hidden, latent, lurk,

but from the irregular
shape-shifter *fero*,

ferre, tuli, latus:
to bear, carry. Ab-

lative's abduction, opposite
relative's return.

Not ablution but ablation's
liquid slipping,

or cutting, away.

Galleria

\

A kind of hangar by the mall.
Propulsive dance hits
looped like the '80s never ended —
B-b-b-b-b-baby, I-I-I-I can't wait ...

A shimmering wall through which
the latest Nikes, Reeboks, and Adidas
parthenogenetically appeared, manifesting
some new sports need — *I've got the power! ...*

Aggressive Vegas effect, indifferent glitz.
No ceiling, no limits.

\

1994. Lights spun
over the towering echelons,
to which we raised our eyes

from The Combat Zone,
i.e., sales rack off to the side
of the main event.

Like adolescence itself
wanna try that in an 8-and-a-half?
(pierced ears, a silver chain,

I was fourteen), threshold
through which all must pass,
where there was no hiding

the rifled-through shoeboxes,
the desperation and shame.
Pierced ears, a silver chain.

\

Out in the night he was waiting
in his pickup — rockdove, bellmetal,
stripped-down primer gray groomed

to a secrecy so irretrievable I can't remember
why he was parked at the Applebee's
three parking lots over,

what happened after I got off,
what concert, if we ever made it.
I see him in the cab, the empty lot

sloping down to the parkway
thickening with the night's traffic.
His look that says I'm lucky, I'd be lost

crossing these deserts without him —
the world's blank patchwork
of parking lots, its power suit

where nothing grows,
nothing retains any water,
running off like debt

sold the world over. *FinalLY*
it has happened to me right in front
of my face and I just cannot hide it ...

He could be Charon waiting for his next
customer, the petty coin of my commission
sealing my shy mouth.

Getting in, my necklace turns to lead,
an x-ray apron holding me
down in the vinyl benchseat,

submerged, let's say,
in a laser light show's
uninscribable fog —
                                        I remember

he had a favorite cousin Sharon,
lived over the river in Huntsville.
He loved to tell about crossing

the bridge once at sunset. Looking down
into the mouth, the very fires, of hell.

Steve's Apartment

    High dive, headlong
open-field hit and hidden
among the uniform brick
of Canterbury Garden Apartments —

    Hangout, hideout, snuggery
tucked away just off
the interstate —

    Just inside the city limit,
a barracks beside
the surrounding estates —

    We always entered by the back
yard between buildings:
back door, galley kitchen,
stack of creaking floors —

    Intimate,
    intemperate,
    impermanent
    apart —

    Lit like a nightclub or still
as a blinkered bar in the day —

    Interstice otherwise
out of reach, out of tune
with the times —

New Wave interval
recognized perhaps
in the wave of your bangs,
you who already knew —

How time caves in
and makes a portal
to lead others through —

He tells again
about Maui Wowie,
Thai stick
held up like a distaff —

Smoking at her loom, a strangely
familiar Arachne, Ariadne
spinning her yarn,
or web —

Young Buck

after Carl Phillips

I looked up and the buck looked up.
I'd come to read where the oaks stretch
almost to the ground. He'd come off
the thick-wooded bluff, or side
ravine with its creek, the creek that made it,
buried by the city.

Maybe six points all told,
like a teen's first stubble at the threshold
of delicacy and strength Steve found preferable,
and why wouldn't he.
                                        How does Byron put it?
"Slender, but well knit." Newly defined
shoulders, the beginnings of a build
relegated for now to the secondary,
ankles turned on a lathe, he was

slim enough yet to slip between
a post and a gate, or, looked at
head-on, to nearly disappear.

The age in deer years a coach said I ran like a deer —
9th-grade baseball tryouts (it was *all* I could do).

Tongue running around his spindly muzzle,
tail down, quivering, he bent to graze,
but before he got there, rose to check
I was still where I was, then dropped his head
again, but not his guard, not — raising up again
prematurely — not all the way.
                                        And so
on and so forth, stuck in his loop,

a needle wavering for how long — each pass
closer by halves — if I hadn't moved?

Andreion

From the Greek
for man. A kind
of hunting lodge.

A honey, lodged
deep. In the woods,
different rules.

A lengthening
of eros, *eromenos*
sounds like ouroboros,

snake swallowing
its tail — swallowing
'men': beloved teen,

pricked with his first stubble,
picked in a ritual
solicitation

and abduction
from his father's house
by his lover,

the *erastes*, which sounds
like harass, arrest.
Soup dribbles

from his beard, while his pet
sucks the soup bones
of their kill.

Cleaning High

He throws his elbow through the gloom,
swirling with his broom
a haze of incense, weed, and cigarettes.
Barefoot, he pirouettes
and wipes the coffee table's grime
like bygone Birmingham
steel mill soot
Gramp said would mark you head to foot.
Mark how lightly his lips hold
their Marlboro Gold,
and how he squints
at dirt piles with a nurse's vigilance.
He's got the oldies cranked, as if the notes
were smoking out the evening's ghosts.
He's opening blinds, a closet door
I never quite noticed before.
Upstairs he bumps around, slamming drawers,
cleaning like Mom on all fours.
My friend and I are slouches
with our notecards on the couches:
case, gender, number, conjugation
and the temptation
to transliterate instead of translate.
Phonemes swirl. We can't wait
to load a bowl. Our one chore
(he sweeps past with hundreds more)
given a lick and a promise
if we're being honest,
if you could raise the blinds
on our one-track minds.
Oh, but we studied Steve
like you wouldn't believe.

JV

The bus back. Some parkway
on the outskirts lit up
of a Friday night.

Homunculus of shoulder pads
beside me, skewered by the bars
of my facemask —

a handle. I lean helmet-flattened
against the dark gray vinyl
of a seatback.

Strip malls peel past. Smells
of bus, sweat, crotch, grass.
Road rattle up

through my cleats and jouncing,
still-padded legs. Star players,
insiders

hang over their seats, conspiring.
In the far back, an offensive
guard who didn't see

a snap is cracking up two rows
of linemen with flamboyant
antics. Evangelical

linebackers are rowdiest and elicit
a grand *sit the fuck down*
from a coach.

Everyone's somewhere else.
I'm halfway to Steve's,
who took the liberty

of offering to pick me up tonight,
his little pigeon-gray pickup
at the edge

of our high school parking lot,
windows down, a glowing
Marlboro.

Sleeveless Steve like it's twenty
years ago and he's waiting
for friends to cut.

"What's up, Muthafucka?!" twangs
from a dad's depths in the cab
to a high squeal,

the bones of his face, his eyes
honed under sodium lights.
I leave

the others to carpool and fool
with truck bed toolboxes,
throw my things

in the back. He slides over
so I can drive. He's fresh-
shaven, light

brown hair combed back, spice
of cheap cologne. I'm as nervous,
he as vibrant

as we'll ever be with each other.
He lights me up as I feel
for the clutch's

deep grab. All mine, a sure thing,
he cranks the Doobies, I bank
a wide turn

toward the entrance, hitting the high
beams as we dip into suburban
darkness

at the foot of Flat Ridge, his front
plate a diver's flag. The air
is azalea

silk, a world apart from the bus
ride's endless intersections,
exhaust and fast

food. He came by interstate
and is glad I know where
the fuck we are,

can't even see the street signs.
I know, laughing my way
by feel

through the labyrinth of deep-set
estates, metal gliding
in the gears

like a creek. We summit, traverse,
and finally sweep down the front
of the ridge,

letting a yowl out in unison, city
lights peeping through trees.
No going out

with me fourteen, so we head to his
place to get our heads right
before he takes me

to a spot he knows in the country.
Friday night, he'd usually
have company.

I can make it out now: he's cleared
his calendar, cleaned, stocked
up on food and art

supplies. While we get high,
he humors me a little
straight, and I

him, gay porn. Do I want to
shower? I can wear a pair
of his scrubs,

his brown sleeveless with the state
of Texas on it. I'm ravenous
to hone the edge,

to know the ledge, like I've jumped
levels in the video game
lighting up

the den, blasting through his stereo.
Beautiful Steve, I want to go
to the trestle,

but you keep buying time, another
glass, another sketch. Then
it's much later

and we're going up the stairs, you're
steering me — a babbling
falls —

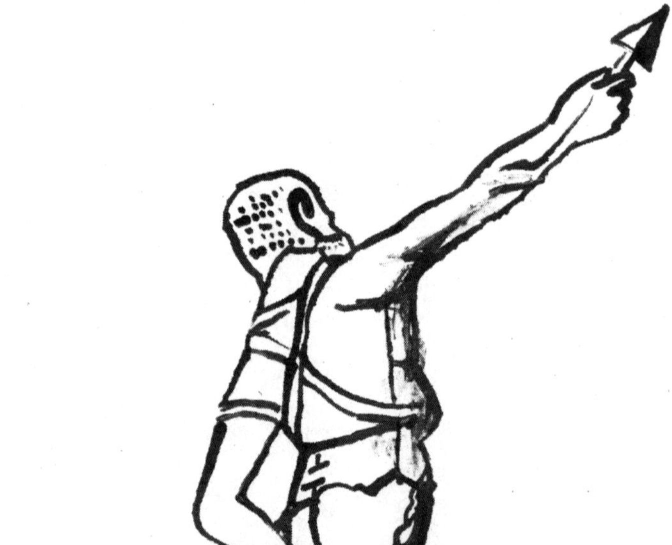

3/

Vulcan

\

From Olympus,
Vulcan fell a day and a night,
waiting to hit.

\

After the World's Fair,
our statue of the blacksmith lay
by the tracks, going to seed.

When they hoisted him up
over the hill and lit his torch
red if someone died in traffic

that day, and green if not, his kingdom
of steel mills, his mines in the hills
were already well in decline.

His limbs were filled with concrete,
and at some juncture the world's
largest cast iron statue had begun
to crumble.
                    As had I,
hours into my first acid trip, fish-eyed
behind the plate glass overlook—

in memory, at least, inside
Vulcan's head. The lights of Birmingham
breached the blood-brain barrier,

crushed between
sleep and her twin.

\

In winter, the ridge cast its shadow
downtown and Vulcan's torch
pointed at the foundry.

\

Who cast the ingot
of Steve’s truck?

\

Who couldn't help himself
from changing the setting, mixing
mischief on a whim. Who was teaching me,
as usual, it all depended,
how much he was needed,
the only one who could,
and didn't —

how everything can be turned
with a nudge.

\

What is vanity but the shadow

cast in the foundry in the valley

of the shadow of death?

\

Finally, it wasn't
truth, or vengeance, but boredom.

The need not to discover,
but confuse, manipulate

and confuse. At the mercy
of variables real and imaginary —

induced, insinuated
just to see.

\

He played with us.
He played against us.

He played us against
each other.

                    The troll inside
the stoplight playing havoc

with the traffic. Up in the air
like Ariel. A Book of Ayres.

Ransack

from Old Norse *rannsaka*, from *rann* 'house' + a second element related to *sœkja* 'seek'

Up and down those creaking stairs
(he wasn't back yet, we'd let
ourselves in), we shook down his dim
bachelor rooms, interrogating
every counter and drawer —
loose keys, an expired ID, beads,
cassettes tapes (nobody we'd heard of),
pantyhose, a wig, a dusty condom.
All we needed was the dust from the bottom
of a bag, and maybe a roach.
Thwarted,
we settled back into cushions still holding
impressions of last night's company.
Daylight leaked around the blinds.
The entertainment system's standby lights
glowed like coals in a clamshell.

A few years back, I'd raided St. Stephen's
sanctuary with a friend — half-pint Vikings,
petty iconoclasts striking matches,
rooting around the chancel and high altar.
We thought we'd help ourselves
to holy wine and don the robes of heaven.
The priest turned up, a sonorous southern

Abe Lincoln, Mom's crush, and smooth as one
        of his sermons, walked us through
an implausible interpretation: our visit
        was really about spiritual curiosity —
like that tale we told the firemen
        about renegade teens burning the woods.

Or maybe, like Mom's knowledge
        of that fire, or of Steve's (how she let me
think I was getting one over on her),
        maybe there was more to it — a deck of cards
from Germany, a flyer for a New Year's party
        at the Civic Center — than we knew.

Lord of Misrule

\

Maybe it started as an accident:
a spot of fungus

in someone's slice of cake
made them hallucinate that they were king

and run around making wild decrees.

And every year thereafter
the baker dropped an anarchic green

pea in the batter —

a suppressed laugh,
a buried pun —

and them who got the lot were crowned
king of the revels.

\

At the appointed time and place, an abdication.

\

A clown with a crown
at the head of the table

at the feast of fools —

in all which space there were fine
and subtle disguisinges

Everything suspect
and everyone subject

that last and longest night,
disquieted and queered —

the only way
to get shut of the year.

The Long Game

\

I should have kept playing
home run derby with Jamie
in his driveway. The *White*
Album, Nirvana, his two guitars.
I should have kept listening
about the Mustang LX,
kept smoking in his room
and old Volvo, stuffing
the ashtrays full. *Although*
we've come, I harmonized
with Corry, *to the end of the road,*
I should have kept being a boy,
climbing in and out the window
to sit on the roof. All summer,
kept throwing junk with an orange-
pink street hockey ball
nicking the trashcan strike zone,
dense enough so that, connecting,
it never went too far.

\

And because I did
because I didn't?

Or didn't
because I did?

_____ is facilitated
but the ground is also being
created for a new _____

The terms are interchangeable.

\

I half-remember Jamie
getting wind of Steve (whom time
and again I went to bat for).
Or maybe, unwitting recruiter,
I let him in on the secret
down the street and across
the golf course, that other world.
He was having none of it.
This guy is how old?

Steve's last bit of advice
was I should move back and teach
English at my high school.
I was thirty and still thinking
it was about me.

Storyteller

\ *Storyteller fountain*

Down the ridge from Vulcan,
a patina-green ram-
headed creature is reading
to a rapt circle:
a wolf, turtle, rabbit, frogs,
a little deer on a dog's back.

This is Five Points, a place to take
a picture, and at night,
to club, buy drugs.

\

After Orpheus lost Eurydice
the second time, I'd forgotten
where he gives up on women and becomes
the first pederast, the first, in one translation,
to enjoy the brief springtime and early flowering
this side of manhood.

\

Every time he told the story, he lost her
again, the love of his life, he said,
to brain cancer.

\

Before setting upon the bard,
those scorned maenads
threw their staffs, rocks,

but, charmed by his tune,
the missiles fell
at his feet.

So the accusations
I imagine our mothers
hurling at Steve

drop, mesmerized before his vaulted tail,
kaleidoscopic feathers
full of suns.

Meditation on the Color Green

In this yet green, yet growing Ark

MARVELL

His eyes when he came home
like a dose of naloxone reviving
lost boys sprawled across couches
in the caves of slumber.

Or, in later years, when I tried
to come around, their disregard.

Pitch and roll of The Country
Club of Birmingham's west course,
where his apartment lurked
over Watkin's brook,
under the 14th hole.

Grotto where the fire god fell.
A sea nymph took him in, he studied
coals in a clamshell,
like Steve soldering circuits
in that factory in Arab.

Green as Ganymede when he found me.
When he dropped me.
Stripling. Princeling. Boy with the keys.

Betrayal

My therapist says a boy with a secret
is easy to control. I wonder how
Steve learned mine, if I told him
in solidarity what happened
when I was nine. Of course, I wouldn't
have thought of it that way.
On the scale of his transgressions, telling it
to a den full of teenagers, hanging me out
to dry, wasn't, for example, one of the many
that could have had him put away.
That I was wrong and deserved to be shunned,
the cause and not the effect;
that he'd drugged me, filmed me,
that the unpredictable cruelties
and disdain that became my lot were the price
of my privilege, I accepted,
even long after moving.
So maybe it wasn't really betrayal
I felt, so much as embarrassment,
when it got back to me a decade later
what he'd done, and how,
a man in his forties, deflecting
for an audience of teens.
Which is why, when I called him up, enraged,
and wouldn't believe his denials or give him quarter
in the long passage of time, why,
since our relationship was transactional,
mortgaged from the start on what happened:
at Steve's; to me —
why his indiscretion could be leveraged,
as long as I could be made

to feel indebted. So he raised
his voice against mine and turned
the blame, before I knew it, back on me.
And when I retreated,
when I apologized, heeled,
he applied the balm, he opened up
the coffers of his attention, inviting me
out to his mom's for the weekend.
He'd pay me to help — his back was shot —
put down pavers by the peacock cage.
Scruffy grad student, I flattered myself
that I was doing research,
I'd capture the voice of the aging
outlaw, the loneliness —
after all those bachelor years —
of moving in with his mom
when his dad passed, living across
the highway from a high school.
Collecting disability. Peachicks
arriving by mail. I accepted
the bumps of morphine, prescribed
for his back, his portrait
in purple over the door
of the shed he built from a kit
to hang out and smoke in,
the same drug administered
at one center till they got shut down
for keeping the old and sick too drugged to leave.
Attar of poppy, crushed under Vulcan's tonnage,
sleep pressed up close to her twin —
they called Morpheus the Fashioner,

and Vulcan, Mulciber, the Softener.
He called his mom Mother.
He was petulant with her,
her rooms spacious and spotless
middle class, galvanized rustic,
whitewashed, inspirational
cursive. He fancied himself
groundskeeper, talking up his pride
of summer flowers, the kiddie pool
he liked to float around in
like a wild eye. Which is why I let him
take me around in his dad's Silverado:
I was being reinstated, remunerated
with a literary opportunity, which,
much to his delight, was already
mediating him, eliding
the cognitive dissonance
of my being twenty-eight
now and living in another state.
In the Salvation Army on the Parkway
I remembered the first time I went thrifting:
Christmas Eve, he bought me a bundle
of sweaters to give my family.
Everyone likes sweaters.
From his Army days, he knew his way
around a drop-ceilinged warehouse,
Lysol scrim and dusty linoleum.
Across the racks, he was in his fifties now,
a bit bloated, glazed eyes like a spouse
on his sarcophagus, speakers
in Electronics piping in

one seventies hit after another
I knew from him. *I fooled around and fell*
in love .... Which is why, lying there
that night in a strange, sterile bedroom,
I felt my howling deficit
in the names of distant townships —
Tarrant, Dixiana, Blountsville, Arab.
And got up, prodded by panic,
and walked past the kitchen with its silver
sheathed from the moon, the hallway
hung with pictures of the husband,
sons, grandkids. *Couldn't sleep?*
he said, when I slid in beside him
in the windowless dark,
keeping to the edge.

Song of Songs

You came like a column.
You came leaping
across the mountain.

Day broke and the shadows fled.

You called through the lattice,
The rains are over.
The season of singing has come.

I wanted to be your dove
in the clefts of the mountainside.

You showed up at my mother's house,
to the room of the one who conceived me.
You gathered my myrrh,

ate my honey and honeycomb.

Day broke and the shadows fled.
A garden locked up,

a spring, a fountain sealed,
I sleep but my heart is awake.

For love is strong as death,
unyielding as the grave,

a stag fleeing fire
on the spice-laden mountains.

Red Mountain

I don't recall his name. We're at an intersection
        under Vulcan: bare ass, a bit
of his fullback's thigh. In the Cutlass
        I'm explaining how I identify
with the year of my car's manufacture:
        1972: Boston, *Cheech & Chong,*
Dazed and Confused. If my parents
        had had me in their twenties ...

He says when he was a kid he liked the '50s,
        says it seems like we fetishize
two decades back. Probably didn't
        say fetishize. Were we on the way
to his place, a condo on Red Mountain,
        a bachelor pad more tasteful and stable
somehow (it helped that he owned it,
        owned the whole building) than Dad's?
Except for being gay, he embodied
        the kind of solidity and security Mom wanted.
He was thicker-set, hirsute, none of Dad's
        stark, vain beauty. And something else:
this safety from a woman's, from my mother's
        terrifying decline.

                                        What happens up there,
the condo stepping down
        in tiers toward Jones Valley, the interstate
and hospital, the railroad and winking
        furnace stacks? What kind of transaction?
He offers me a drink. We take it in:
        somewhere down there under the overpass

lies my last favorite hat, a souvenir
        from my last ski trip with Dad: blown off
out the back of Steve's truck.
        Owner's overlook, hill of privilege,
in all that stoned pleasantness going along
        (where was Steve, anyway?), a moment
of awareness: I could have this.

A Green Thought in a Green Shade

Renting in one of the few apartment complexes
in Mountain Brook precluded Steve
from paying the exorbitant property taxes
that funded my elite education. I'm sorry
to use those words *(exorbitant, elite)*,
but they're what's called for. He knew the game,
kept a bag packed, preached independence
predicated on having parents with assets.
Green man emerging from the thicket
bearing gifts, priapic, his proverbial hearth
lit with the sweet fire, paler than grass, of being noticed —
in time he resolved back into green.
When he steals, even now, into my dreams,
his eyes spiked with vinegar, his highwire twang,
he regards me with the contempt a host
harbors for the one guest who showed.
As if as reward for his theft, discord
had been loosed in the house
where I had hoped care could be kept
under the same roof as desire, joy, mystery, ritual,
like a good education, or metaphysical poem.
As if the heart's green anarchy could be so straitened.

Steve Dancing

As he tilts his head back and spins,
he makes easy every answer:
what to do with your face or arms,
how to dance alone.

His bare feet buoyant, his balance
midbody — it's Chaka or Sade,
it's nineteen-seventy- or eighty-four.

I couldn't come to the New Year's dance,
but off the couch I come along now
for a turn through that otherwhere.

I fawn, I want to drape him like a skin,
as he tilts his head back and smiles.
See, his eyes say, *it's easy.*
You should have seen me then.

Last Pass

after Caravaggio

Half-naked in the gloom,
        the groom is hard behind the horse,

taking risk by the bit. An unseating
        keenly orchestrated, flank and burden,

cover and hoof. It seems obvious
        enough: Saul slumming it in his finery.

The mare assured nothing's amiss.
        Who gets off, who bestows,

who cedes, unseeds, who has a say,
        a gardener, an open flower.

Take Back the Night

\

A disproportionate
amount, did you know,
of night
goes into making
a teenager.
They wear it like a baggy shirt,
shapeless and unfinished.

\

The audio's in and out.
A Stygian mizzle
sidles in under the lights.
Soggy purple
crepe streamers.

                    Projected on a screen,
which a coach — see his feet —
props against the wind,
the founder won't be
content until sexual violence
is "eradicated from the globe."

My job, securing
thin black plastic
table covers with painter's tape
the wind pulls free.
My job, leading off
with a poem.

Afterwards, more
excruciating silence.
A few others answer
the altar call,
wet leaves out of nowhere
turning back to soil.

\

Soggy slogans, acronyms,
oaths, swag have this
advantage: they can't lose
a magic feeling
they never had.
Tricked-out chrome
trim makes a plain
sedan more plain
come morning.

\

At home, in bed,
I rub your head.
Say it was a shitshow.
You'd have to eradicate
humanity.

\

Like the shallow-end
pool bottom
coming up to kiss
a boy's new
rule-breaking front teeth,
what my therapist
was saying, which I
dove off
camera to write down,
wasn't deep:
there was something
very powerful
about being
chased —
no, *it says*
chosen
as the object
of attention

\

In the most important part of ourselves,
about the most important things,
we have been deceived.

\

The year wears the nights
like adolescence.
In the act of a kiss,
in the soft groin sheathed.

\

I know like I know
in the morning
that I love you,
like I love your smell,

that even tonight,
even though I feel
like a fraud,
someone has heard.

Going Back

The crows let go and flew off

one after another when you looked up

and you knew because you were going back

on so much that it was right

You knew because it pricked your pride

and guilt like the wetness

of blood in the dark

that you were going back on all you thought

and it was right

Notes and Credits

The poems in *Groom* work contain excerpts and references to specific works by other authors or artists. Such uses are made and intended as Fair Use of each such work under the United States copyright laws.

The author and publisher provide the applicable attribution to these works based on readily available public information. The author and publishers specifically disclaim any rights, interests, or copyrights to the works referenced.

"On the Road to Damascus": first in a series of ekphrastic poems based on *Conversion on the Way to Damascus* by Caravaggio

"Allegory": quotes "Leda and the Swan" by W.B. Yeats

"Revision": quotes Song of Solomon 2:4

"Steve's Bed": quotes "Dogs" by Pink Floyd (1977)

"Grammar": quotes "The Waste Land" by T.S. Eliot

"Galleria": quotes "I Can't Wait" by Nu Shooz (1985), "The Power" by Snap! (1990), and "Finally" by CeCe Peniston (1991)

"Lord of Misrule": quotes *A Survey of London* by John Stow

"The Long Game": quotes "End of the Road" by Boyz II Men (1992) and *Finding the Raga* by Amit Chaudhuri (2021)

"Storyteller": quotes *Metamorphoses* by Ovid, Book X

"Betrayal": quotes "Fooled Around and Fell in Love" by Elvin Bishop (1975)

"Song of Songs": quotes extensively from this book of the Bible

"A Green Thought in a Green Shade": quotes *Frag. 31* by Sappho

"Take Back the Night": quotes *Venus and Adonis* by William Shakespeare and *The Republic* by Plato

Acknowledgements

Thank you to the editors of the following journals, in which versions of these *Groom* poems appear:

Birmingham Poetry Review: "Brookwood Mall," "Cleaning High"
Blackbird: "On the Road to Damascus"
The Common: "The Groom," "Revision," "Galleria"
Cumberland River Review: "Hermes"
Five Points: "Young Buck"
The Missouri Review (online): "Initiation"
Revel: "Take Back the Night"
The Shore: "City Brook," "Celestial Realm"
VQR: "Anarchist Cookbook," "Steve's Bed," "Betrayal"

I want to thank *Groom's* many midwives: my PTown fellows Philip Matthews, Gabe Kruis, Laura Neal, Sara Martin, and Sophia Starmack; Rita Mae Reese; Jennifer Barber; Keith Kopka; Brokie Lamb; Katy Didden; Jessica Garratt; Meredith Mason; Danny Ceballos; Emmalie Engle; my Dead Recks Angela Sorby, Anna Ross, Claire McQuerry, and Rose McLarney; Keith Phelps; Carly Fraysier; Elizabeth Quinn; Lisa Ampleman; Major Jackson; my therapists, Laura and Bill; my editor, Peter Campion. And my stalwart Ranger.

Thanks in particular to Rita Mae Reese for pointing me, in my own dark time, to Teju Cole's "In Dark Times, I Sought Out the Turmoil of Caravaggio's Paintings" *(The New York Times Magazine).*

> *And when we are there with him, we sense that he's no mere guide. We realize that he is in fact at home in that pain, that he lives there. There's the unease.*

Thank you finally to Emmalie Engle for the magnificent papercut frontispiece, and to Danny Ceballos for the vibrant bamboo ink drawings.

About the Author

Austin Segrest is the author of *Door to Remain,* winner of the 2021 Vassar Miller Poetry Prize and the Wisconsin Library Association Outstanding Achievement Award. Originally from Alabama, he lives in Appleton, Wisconsin and teaches at Lawrence University. His poetry appears in *Poetry Magazine, VQR, The Common, The Yale Review, New England Review, Ploughshares,* and other journals. He was a 2018-19 poetry fellow at the Fine Arts Work Center in Provincetown.

About the Type and Paper

Designed by Malou Verlomme of the Monotype Studio, Macklin is an elegant, high-contrast typeface. It has been designed purposely for more emotional appeal.

The concept for Macklin began with research on historical material from Britain and Europe dating to the beginning of the 19th century, specifically the work of Vincent Figgins. Verlomme pays respect to Figgins's work with Macklin, but pushes the family to a more contemporary place.

This book is printed on natural Rolland Enviro Book stock. The paper is 100 percent post-consumer sustainable fiber content and is FSC-certified.

Groom was designed by Eleanor Safe and Joseph Floresca.

Unbound Edition Press champions honest, original voices.
Committed to the power of writers who explore and illuminate
the contemporary human condition, we publish collections of poetry,
short fiction, and essays. Our publisher and editorial team aim
to identify, develop, and defend authors who create thoughtfully
challenging work which may not find a home with mainstream
publishers. We are guided by a mission to respect and elevate
emerging, under-appreciated, and marginalized authors, with
a strong commitment to advancing LGBTQ+ and BIPOC voices.
We are honored to make meaningful contributions to the literary arts
by publishing their work.

unboundedition.com